THE CANNIBAL COOKBOOK

THE CANNIBAL COOKBOOK

Fiendish ways to cook your friends and serve them right

Lionel Miskin

Macdonald

A Macdonald BOOK

© Lionel Miskin 1985

First published in Great Britain in 1985
by Macdonald & Co (Publishers) Ltd
London & Sydney

A member of BPCC plc

British Library Cataloguing in Publication Data

Miskin, Lionel
   The cannibal cookbook.
   I. Title
   828'.91409   PR6063.I7

   ISBN 0-356-10498-2

Printed and bound in Great Britain by
Purnell and Sons (Book Production) Ltd.,
Member of the BPCC Group, Paulton, Bristol

Macdonald & Co (Publishers) Ltd
Maxwell House
74 Worship Street
London EC2A 2EN

Introduction

Cooking words and pictures in the same casserole makes a very sweet-sour sauce, and you don't yourself need to be a cannibal to appreciate the flavours. If you can take a genuine sage with real onions, you are half way to Blackberry and Apple .... I mean .... Blackhead and Pimple Pie. Cooking recipes are not a straight-forward business. What was Escoffier thinking up when he invented Bookmaker sandwiches or Stuffed Balls and Legs? The mind happily boggles. But this is a Cookbook of the Imagination. And it even includes a few Current Puns. You don't need to take it to a desert island — just savour it over a stiff whiskey.

Wimbledon Mixed Doubles

For this sporting dish of the year, 2 good-looking tennis pears served with ices in large silver cup. Chuck out second pair!

Sage and Onions

Choose an intellectual mould and plenty of good brains. Brainwash well. Then soak in heavy sauce, refrigerate

and remember his Onions.

Sour Kraut

Make no
mistake,
this may
look chauvinistic —
        but nothing sugar and lemon
        wont wash down.
            And have a Lager!

Peers in Syrup
or
Pears House of Lords

Shake tree gently for old, well ripened peers and then add a few life-pears from the nearest supermarket. **Stew** for ages.

Pasta al Dente

You have to be desperate to take to teeth, however well extracted, but a good

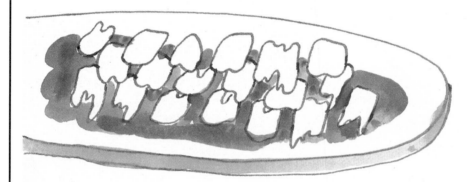

rich tomato sauce provides a nostalgic reminder of the dentist's chair. And the teeth may be safely sucked. Serve brushed.

Athlete's Foot and Runner Beans Marathon

A Marathon can be tough going if you buy a bad foot. Grill a good size 10½ foot with a sprint of mint; run some butter over the beans

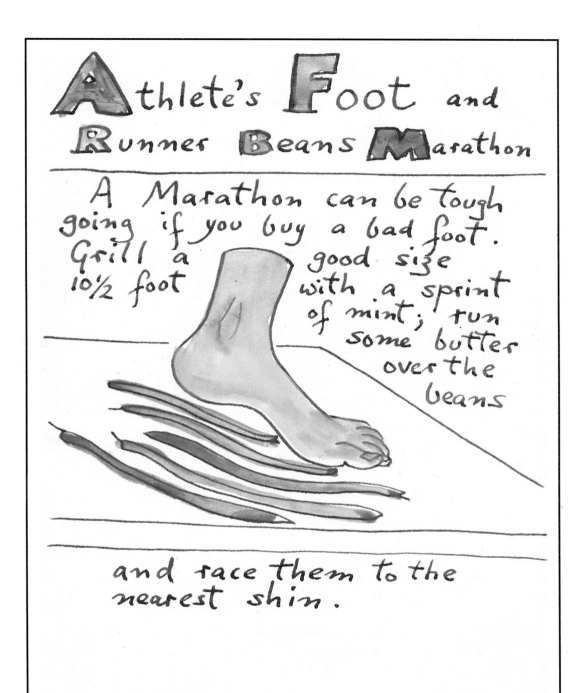

and race them to the nearest shin.

Scotch Brothel

Not a soup, as you might imagine but a collection of tarts on special offer.

May be warmed up but are not to be recommended served cold — even in hot weather.

Battered Babies Bulgariennes

An East European dish derived from Jonathan Swift and a Bulgarian battering.

Use only fresh, fat, and not pickled or nappied babies.

Rape Suzette

If you can't

find a genuine Breton

Rape Suzette, they are not hard to knock up with a good batter and a firm hand. Splendid for pic-nics in deep woods.

Tongue in Aspic
au Tour de Babel

A variant on the famous
Tongue-in-Cheek from Chile.
Keep.. dont discard.. lips,

and if they dont give tongue
when you place them in a
hot oven, twist them.

Fried Face & Chips
with Tartar sauce

Choose fat, flat face
and if necessary ...
pay through the nose
for it. Serve garnished

with lemon and a few
chips off the old
block. Mind the teeth.
To make thick sauce, lipuidize
half a tartar, and salt well.

Dover Soles Immortalized in Butter.

Bastinado the soles well having first filletted and removed tendons, paired bunions, corns etc. Fry corns & tendons separately.

Serve with piping hot tendons, corns, etc, assuming plenty of butter. A genuine taste of the hereafter.

Irish Stew

Nothing to beat it in cold weather. You need at least a dozen Irish. Stew really well. Dont let them quarrel

as you get them into the casserole, and serve with shamrocks.

Apple Charlotte

Present Charlotte well mixed with stewed apple and ginger and if

she needs it, sweeten to taste.

Curried Hot Lips

Red juicy hot-lips in a
rich Madras curry served
with plenty of kisses

and a pound of rice. A
good mouthful ... and
you are away.

Smokers' Lung Molasses Pudding

A cheap, well advertised

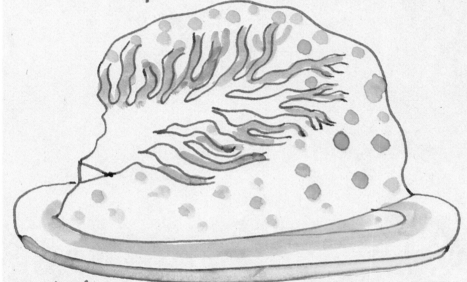

dish, good black molasses provides a substitute for even the most tarry linings.

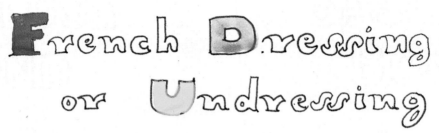

French Dressing or Undressing

Serve with old fish and hope for the best.

Eye Pudding or Voyeur's Glimpses

Into well-fatted pastry place assorted eyes and serve cold in hot chocolate sauce. Have some winking!

Saddle Royal

A™ exceptional Mrs Beaton recipe welcome to all equestrians and T.V. horse-Olympics viewers

Queens Pudding

A gay pudding; add plenty of lib; serve with a giggle in puff pastry.

Pope's Nose Cold or Snotted.

An excellent way to cook is to encyclical the nose in spaghetti

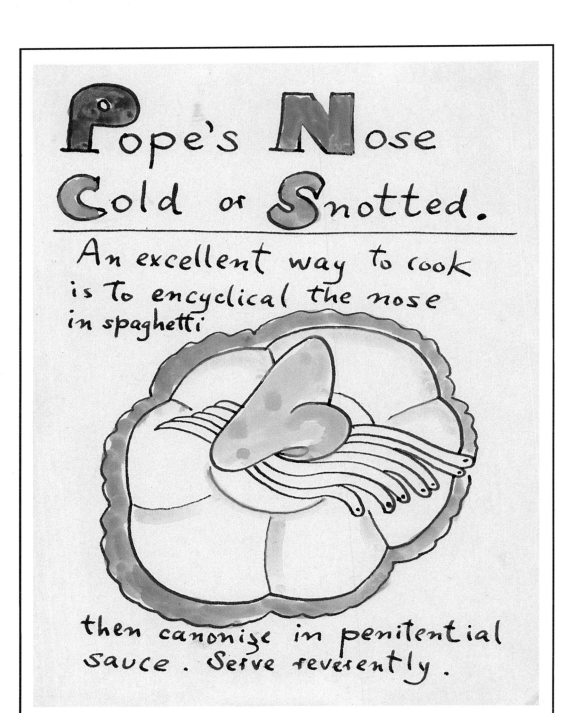

then canonize in penitential sauce. Serve reverently.

Coxcombs and Kidneys à la Grecque

Believe it or not — another Escoffier recipe adapted to cope with any young, attractive males hanging around after the wife.

Originating in Greece, the dish is a favourite now a days among the Turkish community in Cyprus. Extra kidneys make a useful addition.

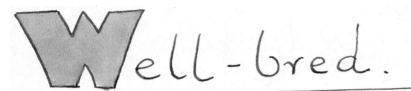# Well-bred.

All but impossible to find ingredients now a days, and

NOT to be confused with a mere loafer concoction like Wry Bread which is available every where.
Half bake!

Strindbergers

Any
three
frozen
Swedes

Warm them up with
a lot of schnapps

Birds Instant Whip

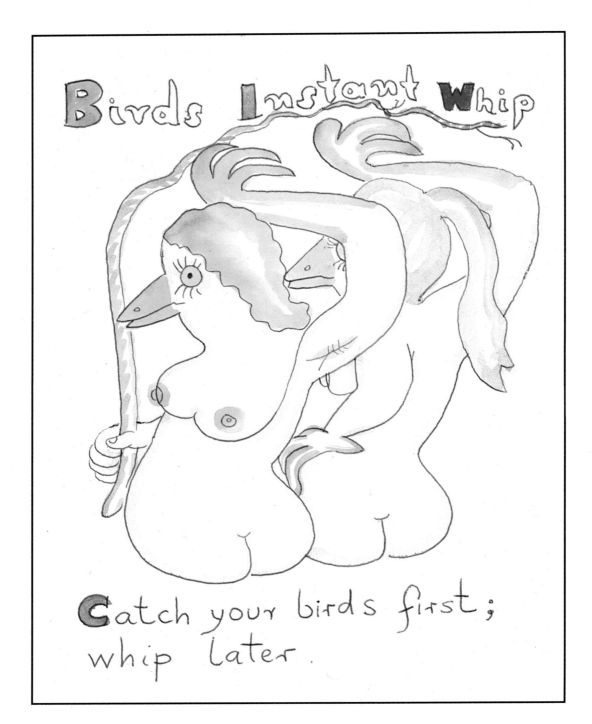

Catch your birds first;
whip later.

Old-Fashioned Humbugs

A kenwood mixer should manage either mint, dreary

or old fashioned hum bugs as available. Spin them for several minutes then watch the same old features re-appear as the grist settles in the mould. Swallow only if you wish to be taken for a sucker.

TOrnados Rossini

One fat soprano or one

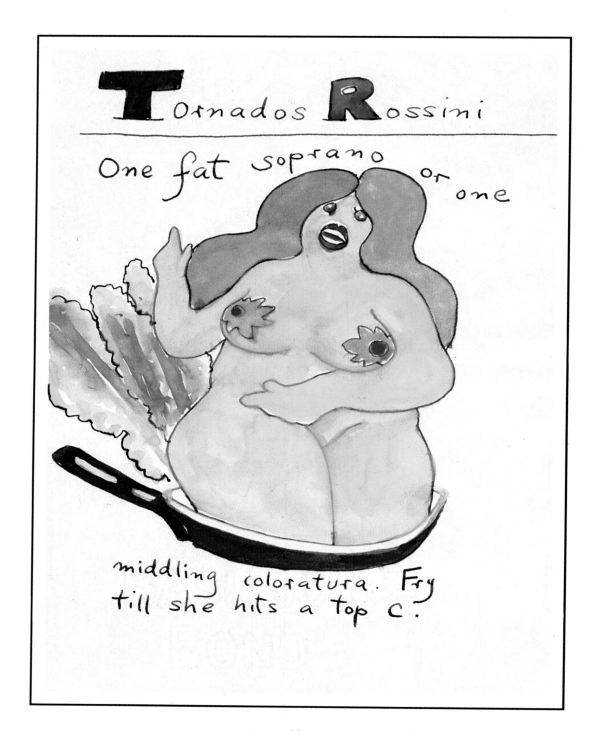

middling coloratura. Fry till she hits a top C.

 Adam's Apple Nipple Ripple

There are many varieties of nipple on sale to-day.

Choose the straight-forward kind and ripple well. Not to be confused with Nipped Adam's Apples.

Devilled Turk

There never has been difficulty in preparing this dish. Simply find your turk and use the bits up.

Pot Belly Pop-au-Feu.

Success depends on stuffing well, finding a big enough pot

and simmering to avoid explosions. Said to be an excellent deterrant to greedy eaters.

Cock-a-Leaky Soup.

To make cocks leak well skewer them after boiling.

Then squeeze onto soup plate from a hight to cool. No need if in Wales to add leaks.

Mastoid and Abcess Sandwiches

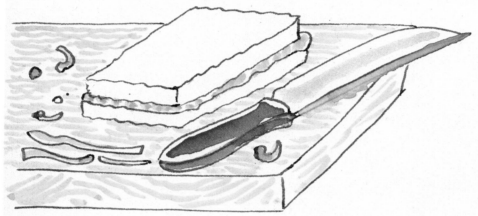

Two or three well-developed mastoids, a quarter of abcesses and bread and butter is all you need for this delicious starter. Salt those from the St George's Hospital well.

Sweetbreads Bon Mamman

Sentimentalists will adore this family souvenir

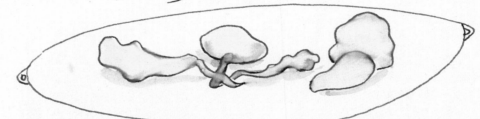

but be sure to boil really well and give father a good helping.

Jellied Achilles Heels

A Trojan dish. Keep the ankles, for they

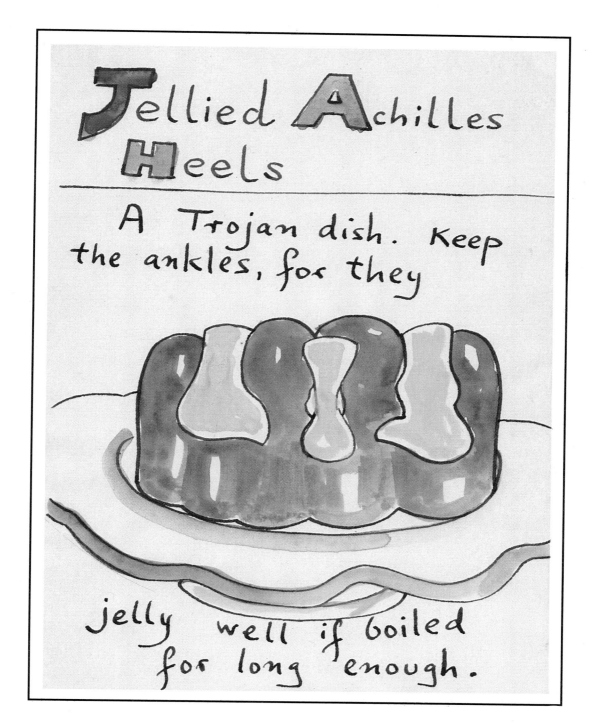

jelly well if boiled for long enough.

Spotted Dick

A good one with genuine symptom sauce beats Spotted Dog any day.

Take care when you lift it.

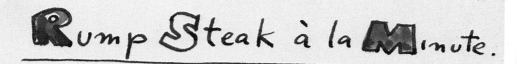

Rump Steak à la Minute.

Take a buttock not too
fatty and tenderize well.
Grill it lightly with a

pat of butter. Serve
with whipped cream
and should be chewed
up well.

Jelly Tots

Fine at birthday parties.
Cats like them!

Christmas Turk Stuffed with Gall-stones.

Surround with roast potatoes and roast for as long as any Turk deserves.

Then baste thoroughly and tuck ... or Turk ... in.

Blancmanged Veins

Originating in a mining area where the work and constant hammering raised the best veins, this cool, slippery dish is a well-loved tonic

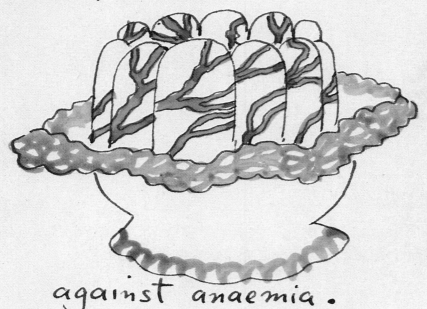

against anaemia.

Tandoori Chick

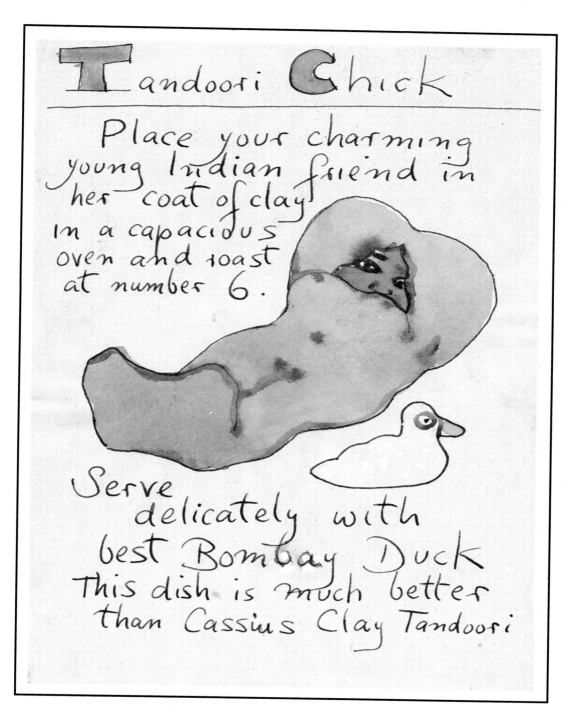

Place your charming young Indian friend in her coat of clay in a capacious oven and roast at number 6.

Serve delicately with best Bombay Duck This dish is much better than Cassius Clay Tandoori

Blanquette de Toe

This dish provides a useful standpoint from which to leap to higher phantasies.

Don't use any old blankets; only MAN-MADE fibres are a suitable base for a pound or more of mature toes.

Scab Salade Scunthorpe

The long association of scabs and Scunthorpe recalls that of

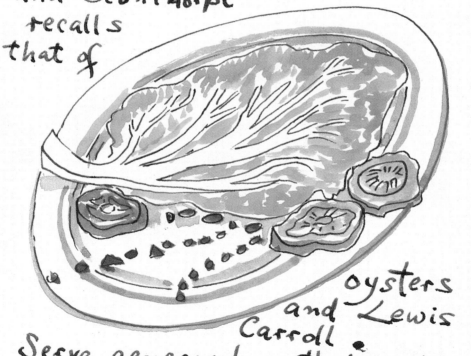

oysters and Lewis Carroll.

Serve generously with tomatos and anticeptic cream.

Nut Meg

An almost vegetarian entrée, comprising any likely old nut-case roast-ed in her own jackets

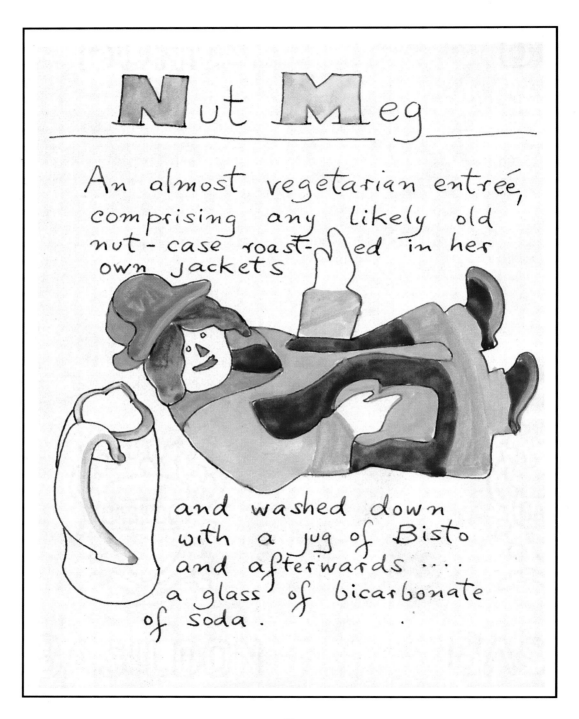

and washed down with a jug of Bisto and afterwards .... a glass of bicarbonate of soda.

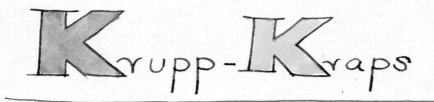

Krupp-Kraps

These explosively fragrant
German biscuits must be
a compound of well-proven

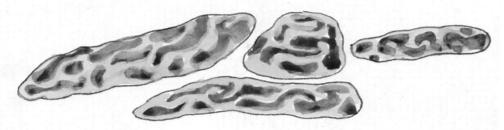

crap and the heaviest
Nietzsche-und-Wagnerwurst
baked crisp and nuttzy
in a really bad temper.

Bookmaker Sandwich

Race-meatings ... are incomplete without your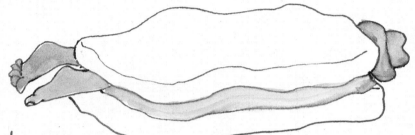

hamper well-stocked with these delicious sandwiches. If you find any too tough to handle, try the bread on your horse. This is another genuine Escoffier adaptation.

Tête à l'Orange
or Tête Bonhomme

A country recipe for

real Head-trippers. Eye the head with cherries and surround with standing PA's-nips and herb the ears and mouth well. Crown with sliced orange.

Ears of Corn

An example of simple country fare, this interesting dish is known as Pasty Ears in

Cornish recipes and was an an alternative filling to meet in MEAT pies.

Thumbs and Custard

Two or three will be quite enough. Be sure they are

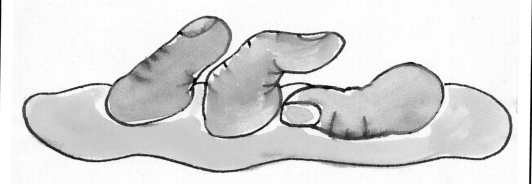

well boiled to soften nails and point them in the right direction.

Bore's Head Tripped.

Ingredients for this dish are readilly obtainable in the staff-rooms of any University.

Remember: stick the tongue out well and surround with boiled cabbage and nonsense.

M·I·5 Fruitcake

Full Marx for 2 or more Cambridge

intellectuals popped into mixed spies with red currants. Serve to Establishment and keep in high places.

Mobster **T**hermidor

Arrest one nasty mobster, boil with

ripped train seats and serve him right.

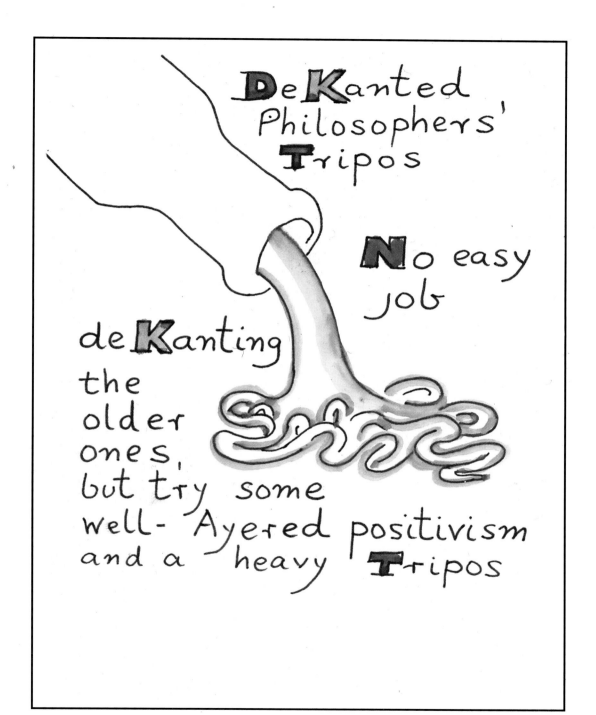

DeKanted Philosophers' Tripos

No easy job

deKanting the older ones, but try some well-Ayered positivism and a heavy Tripos

Stuffed Balls and Legs.

Escoffier's own recipe: These preparations are useful for disposing of any odd legs, parts of the other already of which have legs are boned and stuffed and the skin, which should be purposefully long if this preparation be contemplated, is then sewn up. If they be prepared for serving cold, coat them with aspic, and garnish according to fancy

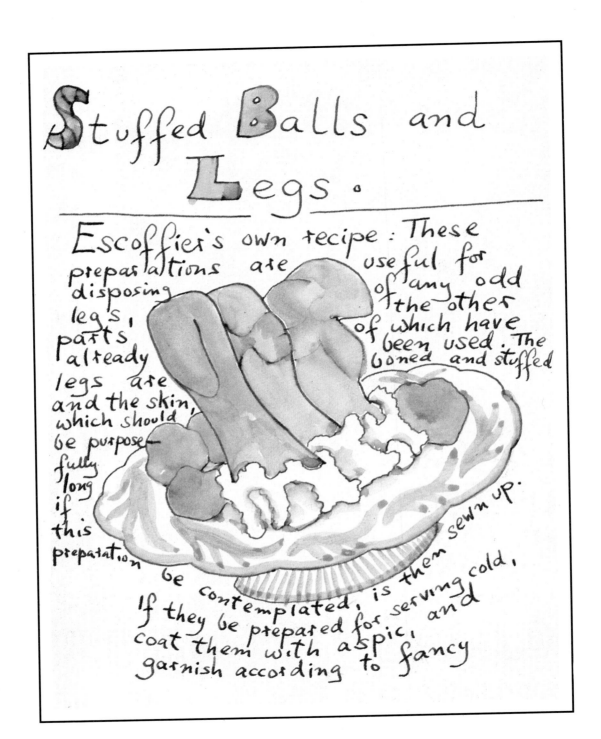

Ginger Beard

Not a drink
but a substitute
for ginger bread
served with a
blank mange .

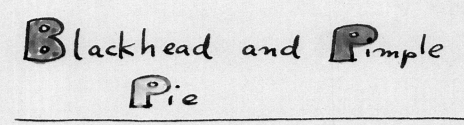 Blackhead and Pimple Pie

You can squeeze a few juicy boils onto the pie

before serving, as this undoubtedly adds to the flavour.

Broiled Surgeon in Scalpels

Lots of money for this operation, a big surgeon and plenty of scalpels.

Eyes Cream

Take a big bite and I scream.

Egg-Heads and Microchips

Chop chips smaller and smaller and keep egg-heads on the boil

Party Sweetreds Stalinated

Soften with a hammer and sickle and splash with bank notes